The Classic Guitar Collection. Volume Two.

Edited and transcribed by Harvey Vinson.
This album was formerly distributed under the title
'Classic Guitar Pieces', Music for Millions Series Volume 63.

Exclusive Distributors:
Hal Leonard
7777 West Bluemound Road,
Milwaukee, WI 53213
Email: info@halleonard.com

Hal Leonard Europe Limited
42 Wigmore Street, Marylebone,
London WIU 2 RY
Email: info@halleonardeurope.com

Hal Leonard Australia Pty. Ltd.
4 Lentara Court, Cheltenham,
Victoria 9132, Australia
Email: info@halleonard.com.au

Cover illustration by Adrian George
Designed by Pearce Marchbank

Estampida.

Anonymous (14th Century)

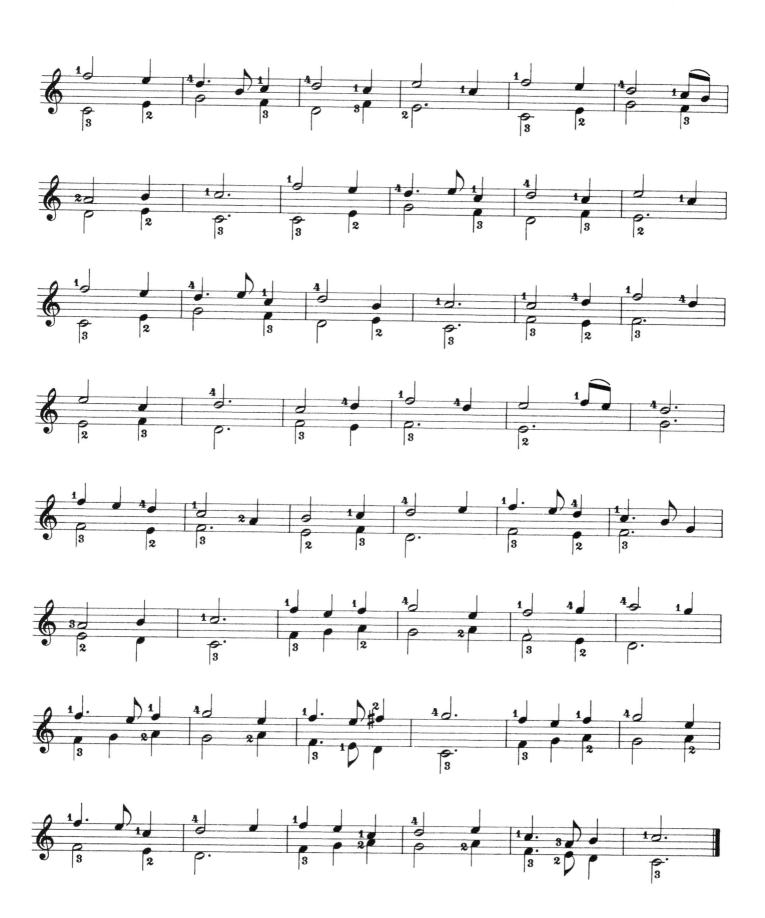

Estampida.

Anonymous (14th Century)

Dove Son Quei Fieri Occhi?

Anonymous (15th Century)

Pavana.

Anonymous (16th Century)

Dance.

Anonymous (16th Century)

Andante

Nachtanz.

Anonymous (16th Century)

Allegro

*This *Dance* and the following *Nachtanz* (Ger. *after-dance*) are paired dances with the main dance in slow suple meter immediately followed by the quicker *Nachtanz*.

Se Io M'accorgo Ben Mio D'un Altro Amante.

Anonymous (16th Century)

Dance.

Anonymous (16th Century)

Veneziana.

Allegro

Anonymous (16th Century)

Passamezzo.

Anonymous (16th Century)

* The *passamezzo* dance (a theme with variations) was frequently followed by the quicker *saltarello*.

Saltarello.

Galliard.

Anonymous
(16th Century)

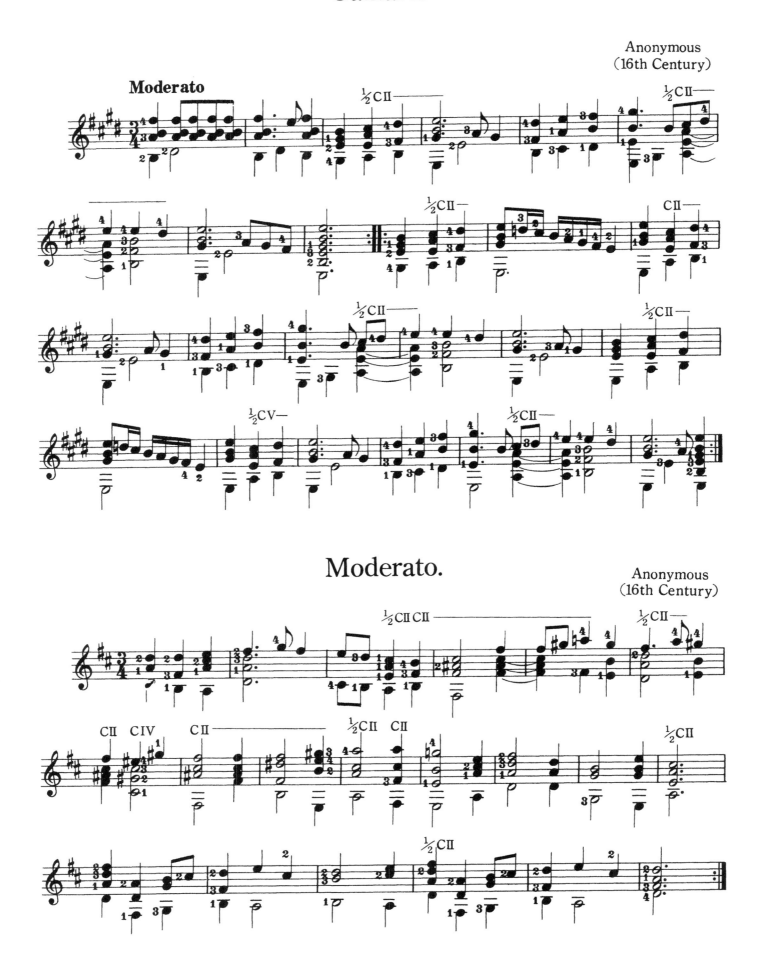

Moderato.

Anonymous
(16th Century)

Courante.

Anonymous
(16th Century)

⑥ = D

Allegro

Passamezzo.

Giulio Barbetta
(16th Century)

19

21

Pavana.

Luis Milan
(1500–1561)

Fantasía.

Alonso Mudarra
(16th Century)

Allegro

*Orginally written for lute, imitates the melodic texture of the harp. Mudarra said that this piece "*es difícil hasta ser entendida*".

Canon.

Passamezzo.

I

Simone Molinari
(16th Century)

II

Fantasía.

Luys de Narvaéz
(16th Century)

Gagliard.

⑥ = D

Allegro

Silvus Leopold Weiss
（1686 – 1770）

Fantasía.

Le Petit Rien.

François Couperin
(1668—1733)

Minuet.

Johann Sebastian Bach
(1685—1750)

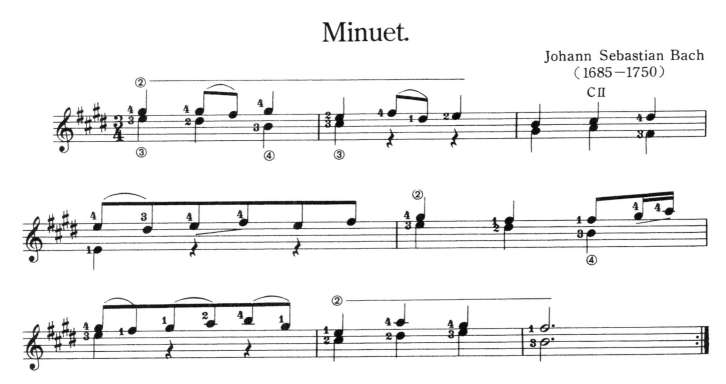

Gavotte in A Minor.

Johann Sebastian Bach

Andante

Prelude and Fugue.

Fugue

D.S. al Fine

Gavotte in E.

Johann Sebastian Bach

46

Fugue.

Bourée.

Johann Sebastian Bach

Sarabande.

Bourée.

Count Bergen
(18th Century)

Andante.

Ferdinando Carulli
(1770 - 1841)

Overture.

Ferdinando Carulli
(1770 – 1841)

Largo maestoso

Introduction

Allegro

59

D.S.
al ⊕

Prelude.

Ferdinando Carulli
(1770–1841)

Allegro Moderato.

Ferdinando Carulli
(1770 - 1841)

Prelude in D.

Francisco Molino
(1775-1847)

Allegro

Prelude in A Minor.

Francisco Molino
(1775 - 1847)

Study in E.

Fernando Sor
(1778 – 1839)

Lento religoso

Study in C.

Fernando Sor
(1778–1839)

Andante

Andante Largo.

Fernando Sor
(1778–1839)

Minore

Study in A.

Fernando Sor
(1778-1839)

Andantino

Minuet in C Minor.

Fernando Sor
(1778-1839)

Andantino

Study in B.

Fernando Sor
(1778–1839)

Tempo di marcia

Study in E.

Fernando Sor
(1778-1839)

Andante cantable

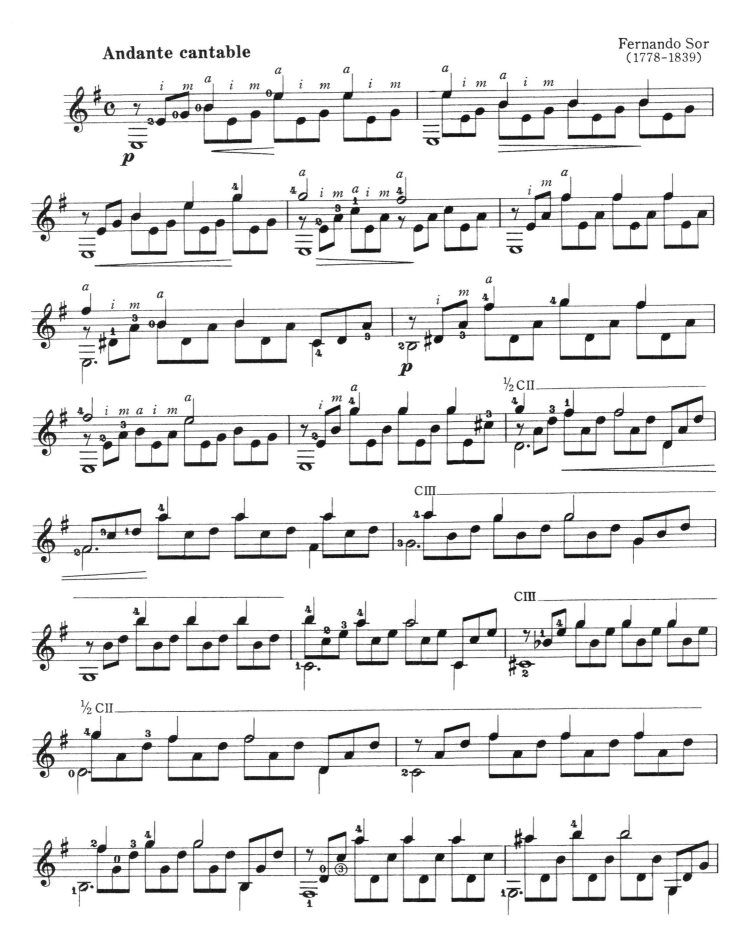

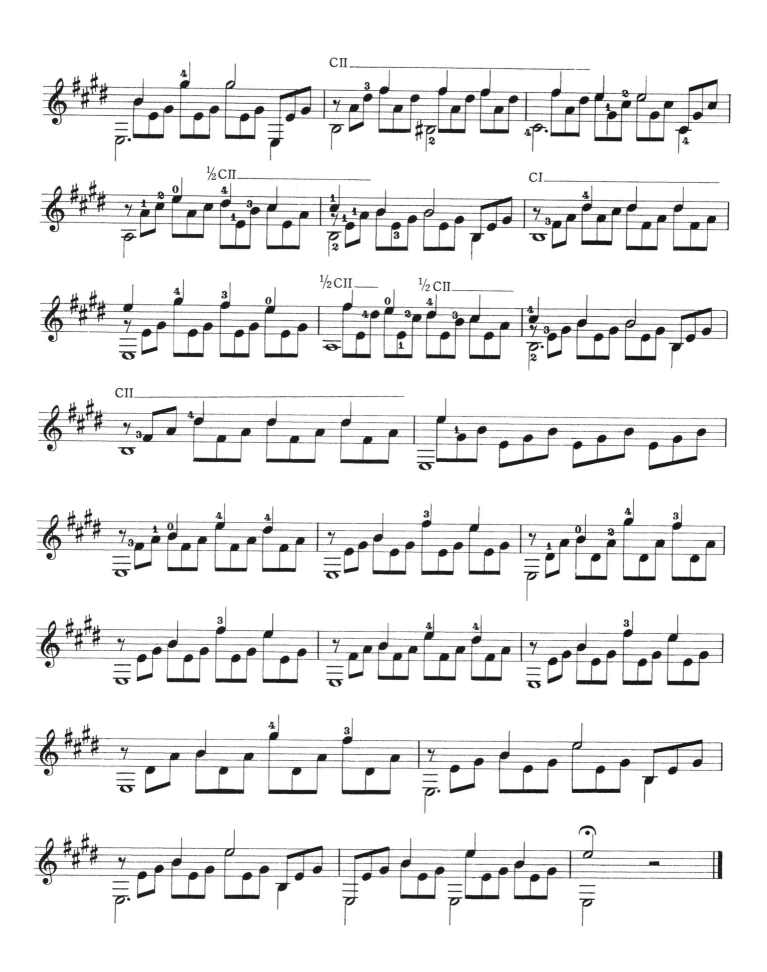

Study in F.

Fernando Sor
(1778 – 1839)

Minuet in G Minor.

Fernando Sor
(1778-1839)

Etude in A Minor.

Mauro Giuliani
(1780-1840)

Allegro

86

Etude in C.

Mauro Giuliani
(1780 - 1840)

Maestoso

Andante.

Mauro Giuliani
(1780–1840)

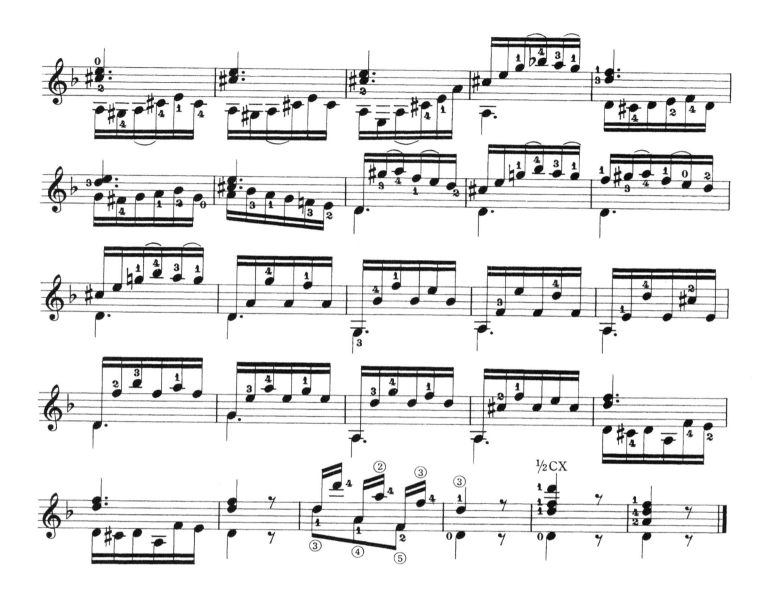

Etude in E Minor.

Mauro Giuliani
(1780-1840)

Allegro

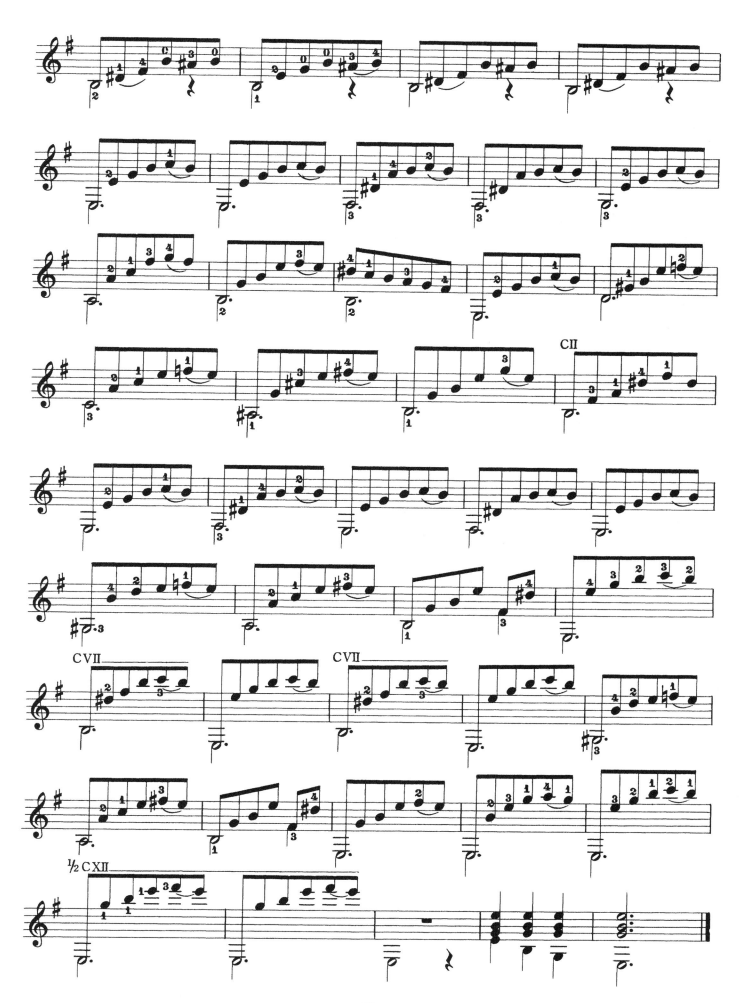

Romanza.

Matteo Carcassi
(1792–1853)

Moderato

Animato

94

Study in D Minor.

Matteo Carcassi
(1792-1853)

Allegro

Study in A.

Matteo Carcassi
(1792-1853)

Allegro

Etude in A Minor.

Napoléon Coste
(1806-1883)

Etude in A.

Dionisio Aguado
(1784-1849)

El Delirio.

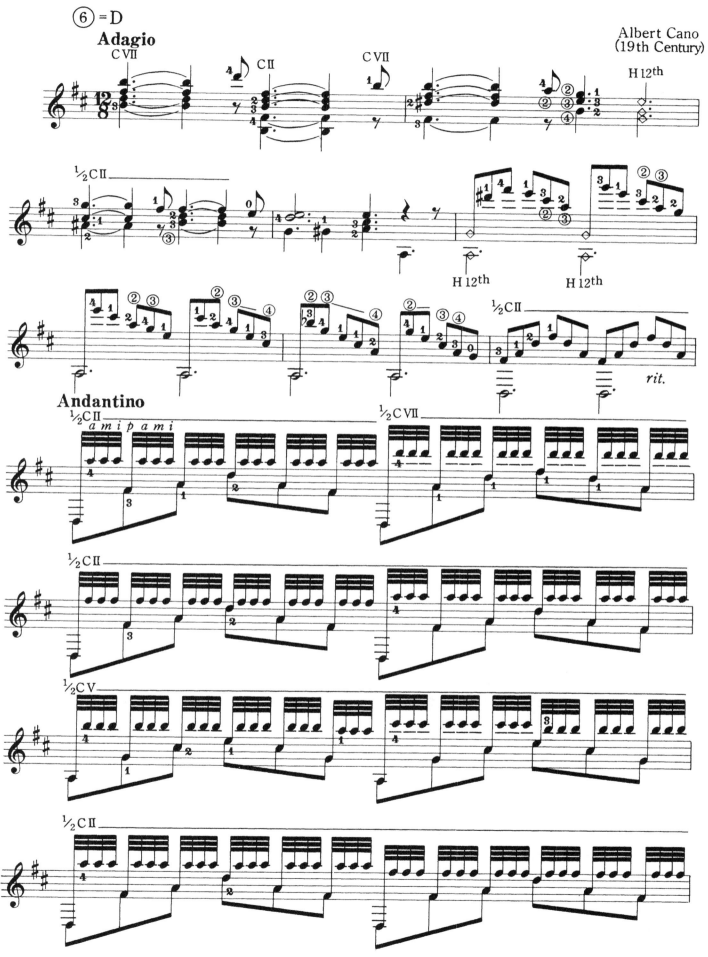

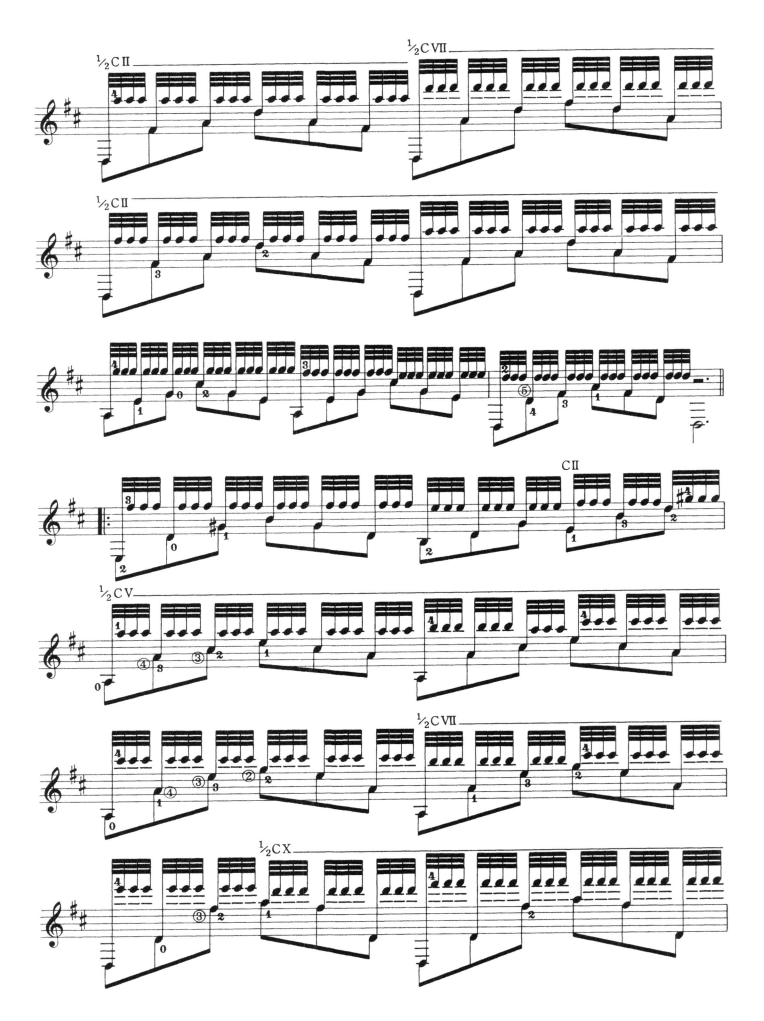

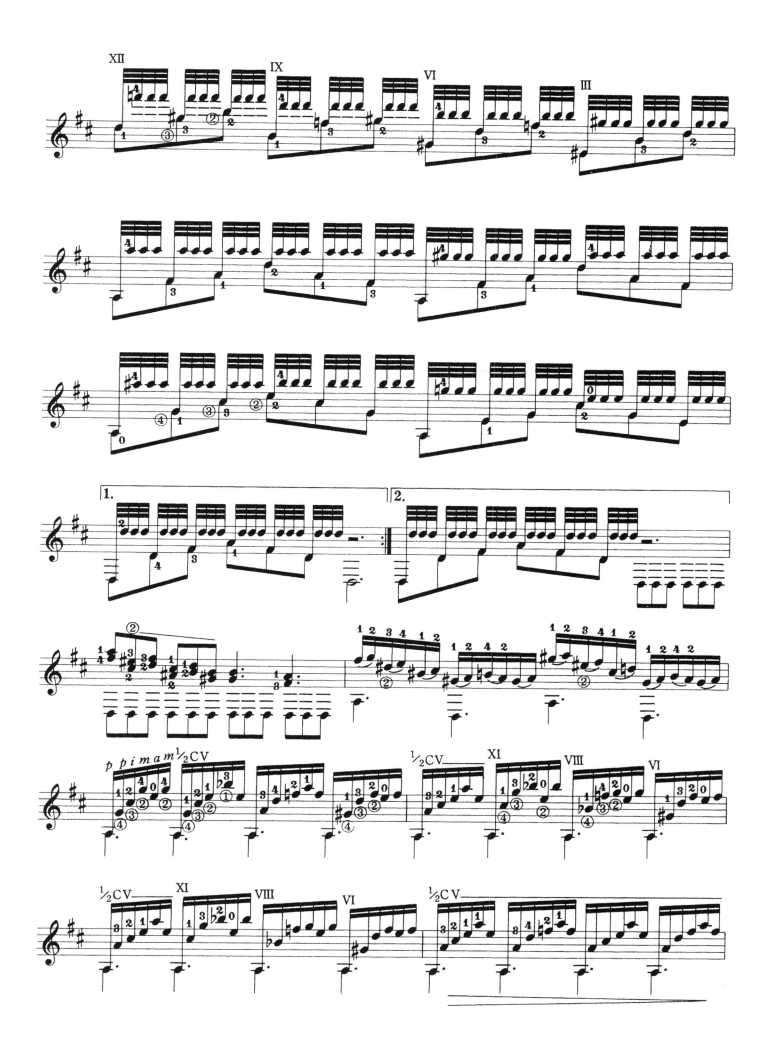

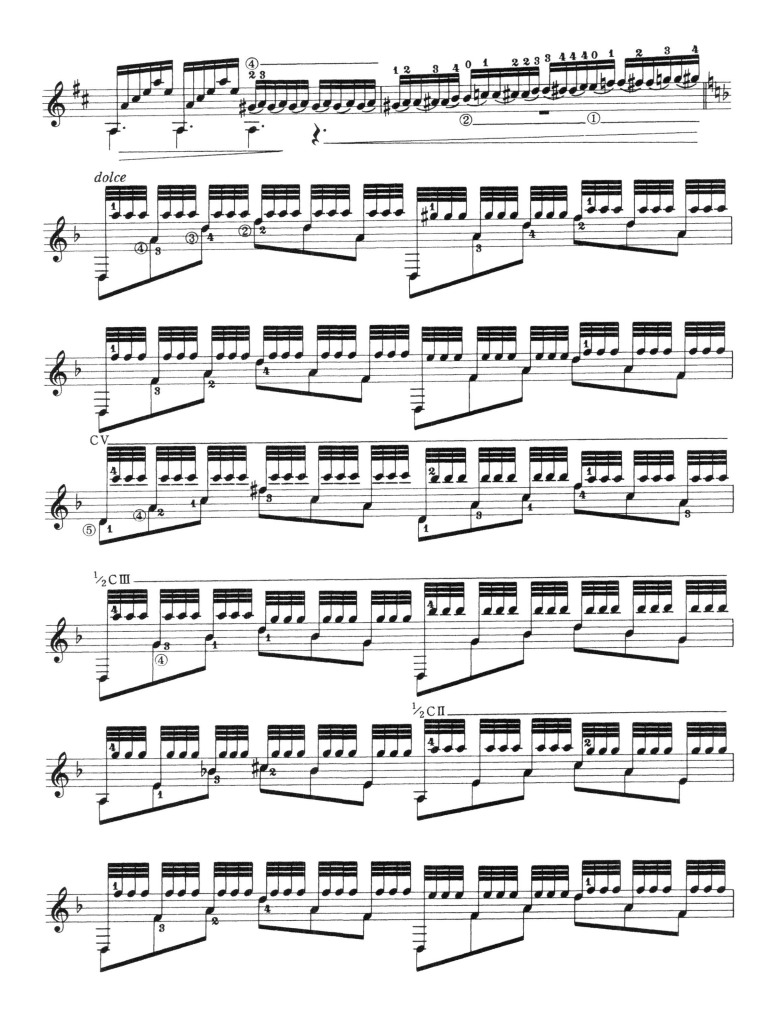

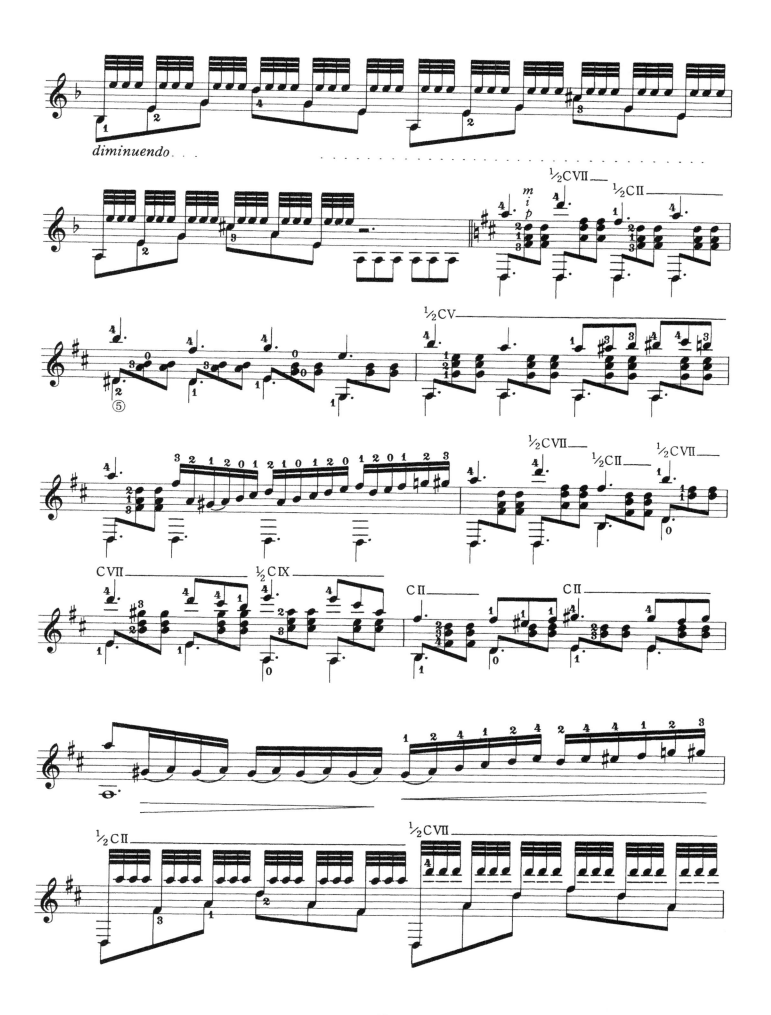

diminuendo. . . .

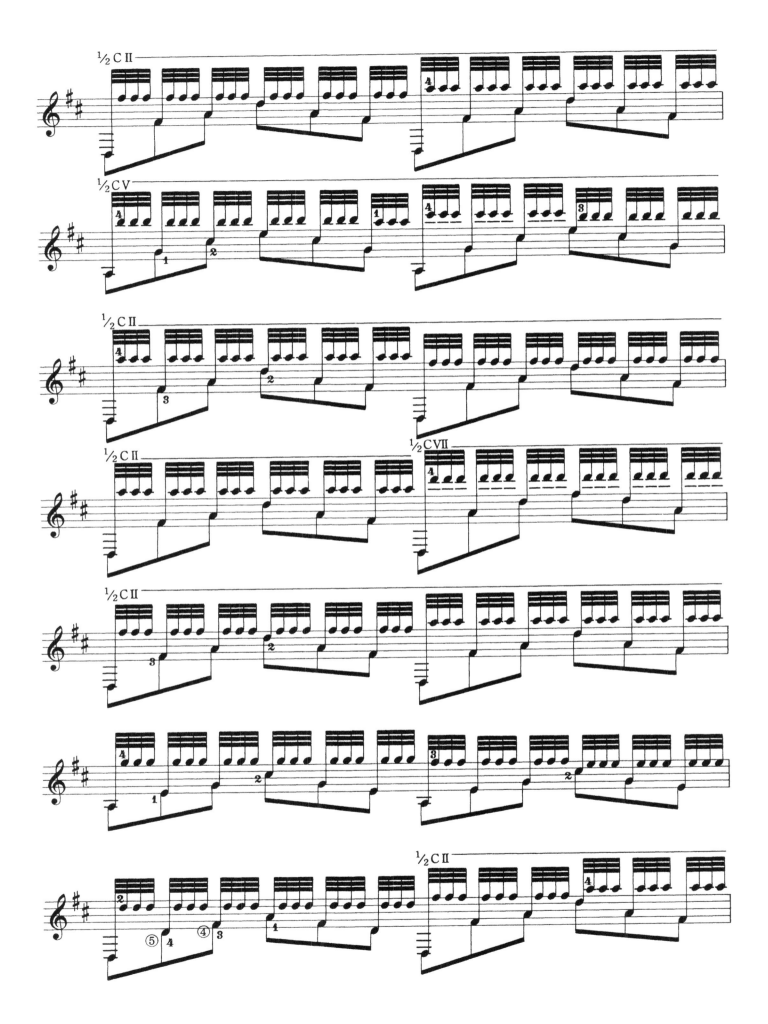

Adagio.

Robert Schumann
(1810 - 1856)

Prelude.

Francisco Tárrega
(1854 - 1909)

Recuerdos De La Alhambra.

Andante

Francisco Tárrega

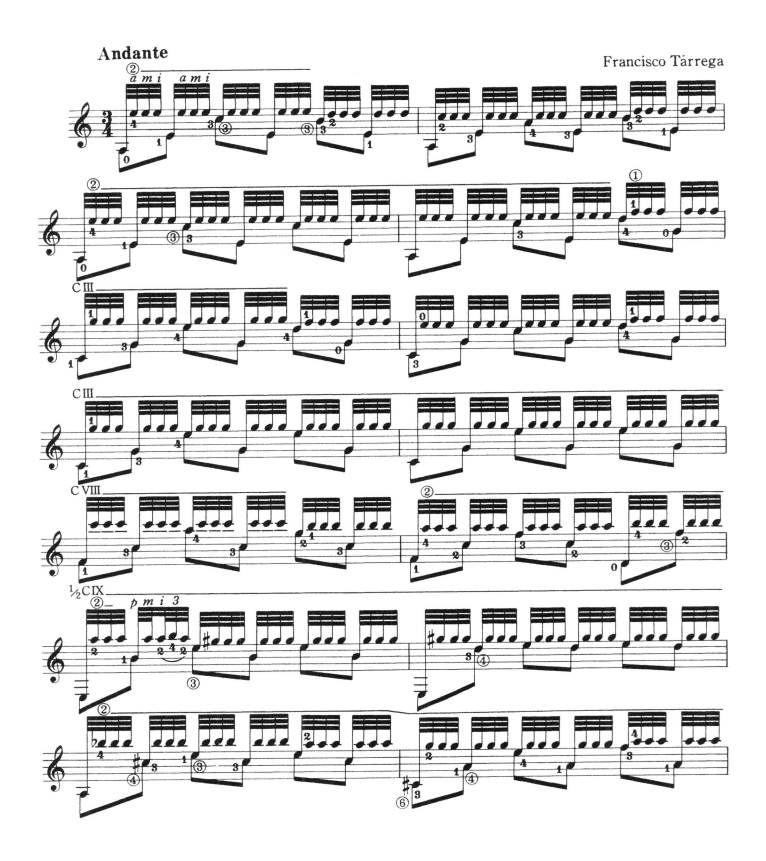

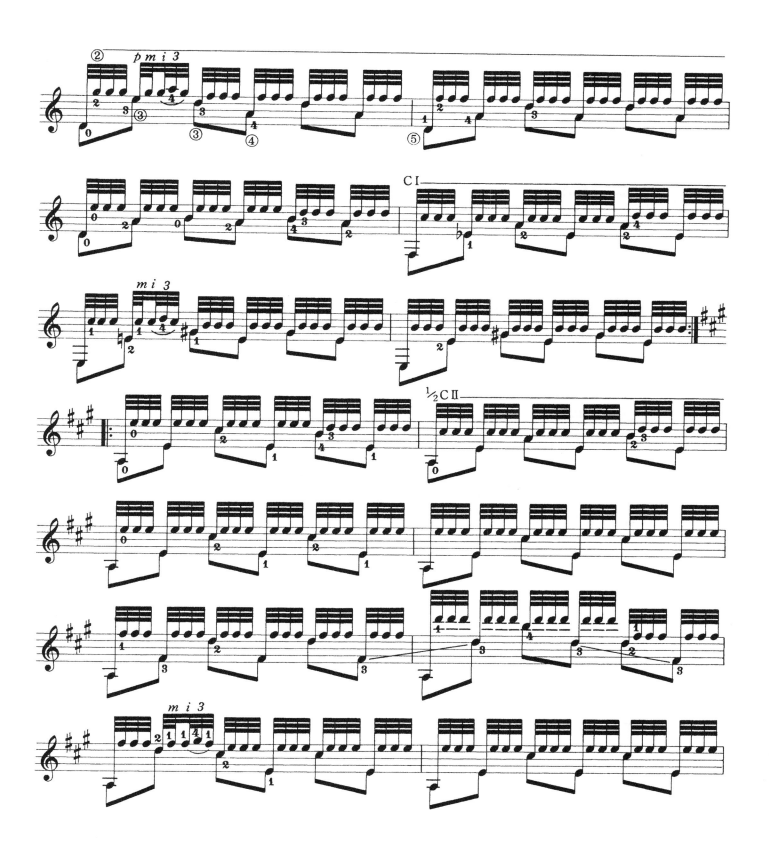

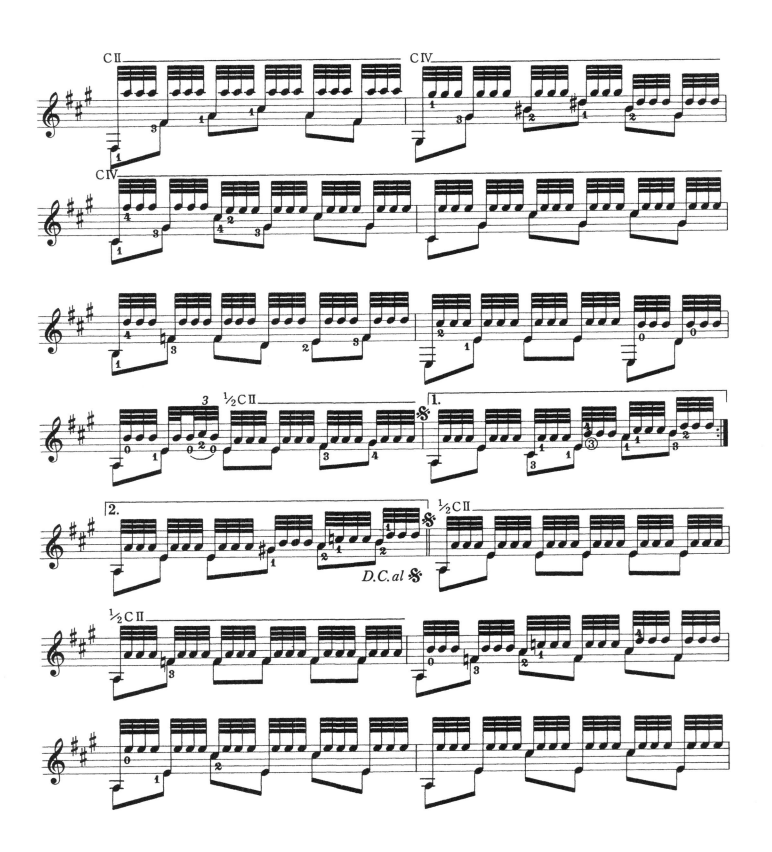

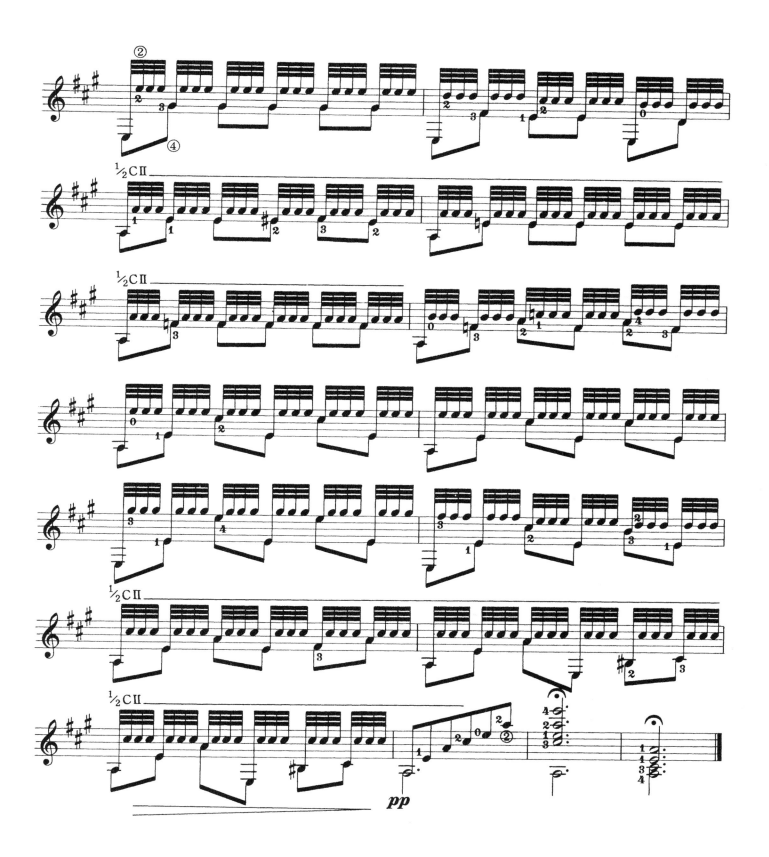

Exchanges.

Quickly & Lightly (♩=120)

William Hellermann
(1939—   )

* *Pont* is an abbreviation for *ponticello* (It.) meaning to play near the bridge. *Nat* is an abbreviation for *natural* meaning to play in the normal or natural fashion (near the soundhole).

Chanson.
(from Episodes for Piano)

Alexandre Tcherepnine
(1899 —   )

When I Get Home.

Elizabeth Cotton
（20th Century）

Adapted by Elizabeth Cotton

Wilson Rag.

Elizabeth Cotton

March.

Dmitri Shostakovich
（1906－1975）

Allegro

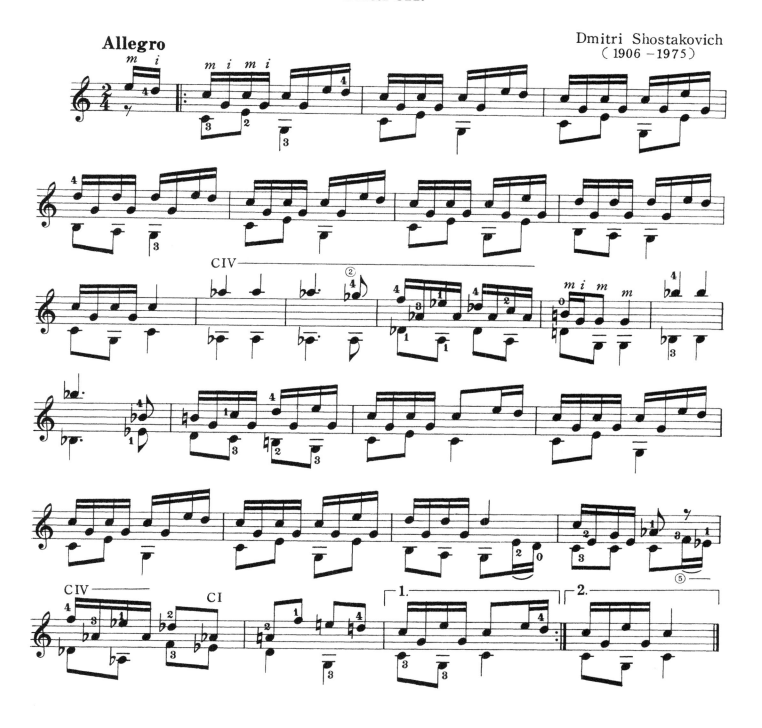

An Easy Piece Using Five Notes.

Igor Stravinsky
(1882–1971)

Song.

Moderato

John Mustang
(20th Century)

American Flag Rag.

Miniature.
(from For Children)

Béla Bartók
（1881–1945）